UNSTUCK

A Motivational Guide to Overcoming Procrastination

Break Free from Procrastination & Become the Person
You Were Meant to Be

By: Katakam

Preface

Better Self

You know what you need to do—but somehow, you keep putting it off. The to-do list grows, and so does your guilt. In **Unstuck**, Katakam weaves together transformative real-life stories, practical psychology, and powerful exercises to help you not only beat procrastination but rebuild your mindset from the inside out. Each chapter includes storytelling, worksheets, affirmations, and step-by-step actions that guide you toward lasting change.

This is more than a book—**it's your blueprint for a better self**.

Contents

Chapter - 1
The Lie Of Later

Later Rarely Comes

Gokul stared at the blinking cursor on his laptop screen, the essay deadline just hours away. The cold blue light of his desk lamp reflected in his tired eyes, yet his hands remained still. He had told himself he would start after dinner. Then after checking Instagram. Then after one more YouTube video. Now it was nearly midnight. Panic was finally louder than his excuses, but still, he couldn't begin.

His story isn't unique.

We all have a Gokul inside us—someone who wants to achieve something meaningful but is paralyzed by the fear of starting. For Gokul, the essay was just one of many unfinished tasks. Gym plans, job applications, a podcast idea, even texts he never replied to—they all piled into a silent mountain of guilt that pressed on his chest every morning. The more he delayed, the heavier the weight became.

Across town, Gokul's older sister Sunita was burning the midnight oil too—but for a very different reason. She had built a small business from scratch, selling handmade journals online. What started as a procrastination hobby during her college finals had now become a thriving side hustle. Her secret? She didn't wait to feel ready.

When Gokul finally called her, voice shaky, she didn't scold him. Instead, she said, "You're not lazy, Gokul. You're scared."

Those words cracked something open in him.

"What if I fail?" he whispered.

"You already are," she replied gently. "By not trying."

At that moment, something shifted. Not completely, but enough to consider that procrastination wasn't about laziness—it was about fear. Fear of failure. Fear of imperfection. Fear of beginning without knowing how it'll end.

This book begins here, with Gokul. With all of us who have been Gokul. Because procrastination isn't a flaw in your character—it's a response. A habit. A defense mechanism. And like all habits, it can be rewired.

You don't need to transform your life overnight. You just need to take one honest step today. Even reading this page counts.

Because the biggest lie procrastination tells you is this: "Later is better."

But later rarely comes. — Let's begin now.

Name the Fear

The next morning, Gokul sat on the park bench near his apartment, phone in hand, replaying the conversation with Sunita in his mind. The autumn air was crisp, and the world felt slower somehow—like even time had taken a breath. He tapped a few notes into his phone, fragments of thoughts that didn't yet make sense. *"Fear isn't weakness,"* he typed, *"It's a signal."*

Later that day, Sunita sent him a message: *"Read this when you're ready."* Attached was a voice note.

"Gokul," her voice said warmly, "Most of us think procrastination is about time management. It's not. It's about emotional management. We avoid tasks that bring discomfort—uncertainty, criticism, effort, risk. We delay the things that matter most because they touch the parts of us that feel most vulnerable."

Gokul paused the recording and stared at the sky. It made sense. He wasn't putting things off because he was lazy. He was trying to protect himself. From what, though? From failure? From judgment? From disappointing himself?

He pressed play again.

"... and the more you avoid something, the scarier it gets. That email you didn't respond to becomes a mountain. That gym session you skipped becomes guilt. That idea you sat on becomes regret. The brain loves familiarity—even if that familiarity is failure. But you can teach it a new pattern."

That night, Gokul sat at his desk again—but this time with no laptop. Just pen and paper. He drew a line down the middle of the page and labeled the columns: *'Tasks I'm Avoiding'* and *'What I Fear Will Happen If I Do Them.'*

His list grew quickly:
- ➔ *Apply for that internship | Fear of rejection*
- ➔ *Call Mom back | Fear of emotional conversation*
- ➔ *Begin podcast outline | Fear of not being good enough*
- ➔ *Finish essay | Fear of failing the class anyway*

Just seeing the fears written down brought a strange sense of relief. They weren't monsters under the bed anymore. They were just... thoughts. And thoughts could be challenged.

That's when Sunita called.

"I know what you're doing," she laughed. "You're dissecting your own mind."

"I think I'm more afraid of success than failure," Gokul admitted. "If I start, I have to keep going. What if I can't?"

Sunita's tone softened. "Then you'll rest. But you won't quit. There's a difference."

That line settled deep into his bones. He didn't have to be perfect. He didn't have to be fast. He just had to be honest—with himself.

And honesty meant starting even when it felt scary. Especially then.

Because fear isn't a red light—it's a green light with resistance.

> ❖ **Key Insight:**
>
> *Avoidance is a signal, not a character flaw. When we identify what we're truly afraid of behind each task, we reclaim our power to move forward—not with pressure, but with clarity.*

❖ Worksheet: What Are You Avoiding?

Make your own list with two columns:
1.   Tasks You're Avoiding
2.   What You Fear Will Happen If You Do Them

Then ask yourself: What's the worst-case scenario? And what's the best?

❖ Affirmations:

Close your eyes and repeat in your mind
→   "I am not my fear."
→   "Taking action quiets my anxiety."
→   "I face discomfort with courage."

❖ Journal Prompt:

Write about one thing you've been avoiding and the real reason why. Be honest. What would it feel like to start—even if it's just 5 minutes today?

Three Minute Identity Reset

Two days later, Gokul met Sunita at a quiet café near the university library. She had a leather-bound notebook open, a latte in one hand, and a familiar smirk on her face.

"You've been journaling," she said before he even sat down.

He chuckled. "It's weird how just writing stuff makes my brain... breathe."

"That's because it externalizes your chaos," she replied, sliding her notebook toward him. "And when you look at it on paper, it loses its power."

Gokul scanned her pages—lists, reflections, bold statements circled like battle cries: *'I do hard things. Discomfort is the path. Progress is louder than perfection.'*

He flipped to a clean page and borrowed her pen.

"What are you writing?" she asked.

"Not sure yet," he replied, staring at the blank page. "But I think I need to write down who I've been acting like... and who I actually want to become."

This idea of identity was new to him. He had always thought procrastination was about discipline—getting things done. But now, he saw it was deeper. It was about the story he told himself.

Sunita leaned forward. "Let me show you something."

She drew a triangle and labeled the corners:

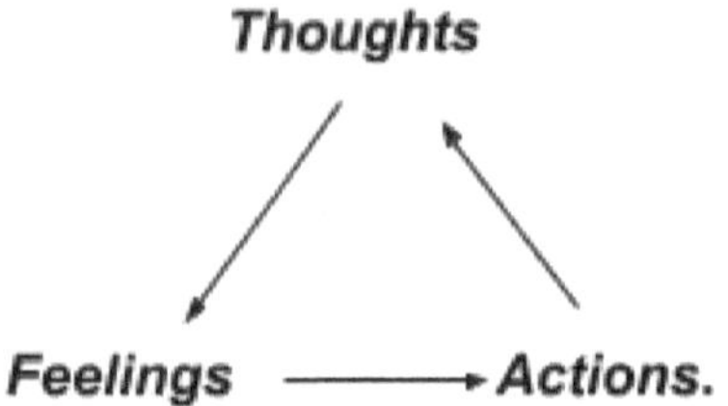

"This is the loop," she said. "Your thoughts create feelings. Feelings drive actions. And your actions reinforce your thoughts. If you think you're lazy, you feel guilty. Guilt makes you avoid. Avoidance confirms you're lazy."

Gokul sat back, stunned. "So to break the loop... I have to change the thought?"

"Exactly," she nodded. "Even if it feels like a lie at first."

He scribbled in his notebook: *'I am consistent. I am capable. I follow through.'*

It felt awkward. Fake, even. But also... like a door opening.

That night, Gokul created a daily ritual. He called it his "3-Minute Identity Reset." Every morning, before checking his phone, he would write one affirmation, one small action, and one reason why he mattered.

Day 1:
- **Affirmation:** "I finish what I start."
- **Action:** Write the first paragraph of my essay.

- **Why I matter:** Because I bring stories to life.

He didn't wait to feel motivated. He simply showed up.

By the end of the week, he hadn't just started his essay—he had outlined the entire podcast series he'd been dreaming about for months.

Each micro-win rewired the narrative in his head.

And slowly, the story of a forgetful, inconsistent procrastinator was being replaced by someone who took small, brave actions daily.

> ❖ **Key Insight:**
>
> *Identity shapes action more than willpower. When we speak to ourselves like the person we want to become, even small actions—done consistently—can rewire our self-belief.*

❖ Worksheet: The Identity Reset Loop

1. Write one thought you want to believe about yourself (even if it feels untrue).
2. Identify one small action that aligns with that belief.
3. Complete this sentence daily: **"I matter because..."**

❖ Affirmations:

→ "I show up even when I don't feel ready."
→ "My identity is shaped by my choices."
→ "Every small action is a vote for the person I'm becoming."

❖ Journal Prompt:

What is a false belief you've been telling yourself? What action today can begin to rewrite that belief?

Rewiring the Loop

Gokul sat cross-legged on his bedroom floor, headphones in, listening to a podcast episode Sunita had sent him titled: *"Procrastination Isn't a Time Problem—It's a Brain Pattern."*

The host's voice was calm, clinical, but compassionate.

"When you procrastinate, you're not being irrational. You're protecting yourself," the speaker said. "The brain registers a hard task as a threat. It wants you to feel safe. So it redirects you toward pleasure—scrolling, snacks, Netflix—anything that releases dopamine quickly."

Gokul paused the audio.

So his brain wasn't broken. It was doing what it thought was right.

But that survival instinct, left unchallenged, had cost him years.

Later that night, he called Sunita again. "Okay," he said, "I get the science now. But how do I override it?"

She smiled. "You don't override it. You re-train it."

He raised an eyebrow. "With what? Force?"

"No," she said. "With safety. And proof."

She explained that each time he completed a small task—even a ridiculously easy one—his brain stored it as evidence: *I can do hard things and nothing bad happens.*

Over time, the brain begins to associate challenge with confidence instead of fear.

She called it the **Micro-Bravery Method**.

Here's how it worked:

1. **Pick a Task That Intimidates You.** (Example: outlining a presentation)

2. **Break It Into Micro-Steps.** (Step 1: Open the doc. Step 2: Title it. Step 3: Brain-dump ideas.)

3. **Reward the Completion.** (A positive word, a journal entry, or even a stretch break.)

4. **Repeat Daily.**

Gokul scribbled the steps into his journal, labeling them: *"How to Rewire My Brain."*

The next morning, he tried it.

His micro-task? Just *open* his essay file and *write one sentence.*

He did. And something weird happened.

He wrote a second.

And then a third.

Fifteen minutes passed before he looked up. For the first time in weeks, he had lost himself in the flow. Not because he was inspired. Not because he was motivated. But because he had told his brain: *We're safe. Let's do this together.*

When he called Sunita later, his voice was giddy.

"I tricked myself into writing!" he said. "Like some kind of mental jujitsu."

She laughed. "You didn't trick yourself. You gave yourself permission."

That night, Gokul added a new section to his notebook: *Neuro Notes.*

❖ **Key Insight:**

Your brain isn't sabotaging you—it's trying to protect you. But by pairing small, safe actions with intentional habits, you can retrain it to associate discomfort with growth, not fear.

❖ **Worksheet: The Micro-Bravery Method**

- Task that intimidates me: ___________________
- Micro-step I can do today: _________________
- My small reward will be: __________________

Use this daily to build up your brain's evidence bank that *you take action—even on hard things.*

❖ **Affirmations:**

- "I teach my brain that challenge is safe."

- "I do one brave thing each day."

- "Progress rewires my patterns."

❖ **Journal Prompt:**

What task have you avoided because it felt overwhelming? Break it into the smallest step possible. What could shift if you did that one step today?

Begin Before You're Ready

Gokul sat with his feet in the river, the late afternoon sun turning the water into streaks of gold. The sounds of birds and distant traffic blended into the kind of silence that invites clarity.

He opened his notebook and began to write—not because he had to, but because something inside finally wanted to.

He wrote about the fear of being seen trying. The fear of starting and failing publicly. The fear of beginning something he might not finish. But more importantly—he wrote about how those fears had lost their power the moment he took control.

Then he flipped the page and scribbled three words in all caps: **"NOW > LATER."**

At the same time, somewhere in a quiet room across the city, I (Katakam, the author of this book) stared at an empty document on my laptop screen lighting the whole room with its bright blankness.

I remember it clearly.

There was a day when I told myself: *"I'll do it when I'm ready."* I had a dream— writing a book, building a startup, a version of myself that I could almost see—but fear built a glass wall between me and the dream. I kept reaching, but never broke through.

It wasn't laziness. It was fear wearing a thousand clever disguises.

And then one day, I chose to do **one small thing**. Not a perfect thing. Not a big thing. Just one brave thing.

Just started writing a word on this blank document that I was staring at. A word became a sentence, the sentence became a page. But it was **the moment everything began to shift**.

I learned that transformation doesn't begin with clarity—it begins with **courage**.

This courage, like a wildfire, burnt my fears and made me take the steps towards my Startup that was waiting for me to start. I took consistent, regular small steps, one action at a time, towards my idea. Now as I'm writing this page, I've already launched my Startup, started impacting thousands of people's healths positively and empowering many farmers and women from villages.

I stopped waiting for later.
And started becoming the person I'm meant to be—**one action at a time.**

That's what this book is about.

It's not a lecture. It's a **mirror**.
A place where your old patterns meet new possibilities.
Where your past delays meet future decisions.
Where you realize that you don't need to be ready—you just need to be **willing**.

Just like Gokul.

Just like Katakam.

Just like every single person who has ever stood on the edge of change and chosen to leap.

❖ **Key Insight:**

Transformation begins when you stop waiting to feel ready and start acting in alignment with who you want to be. Small, consistent steps create identity, not motivation alone.

❖ **Transformation Plan: The Now List**

Write your personal "NOW" plan:

1. One task I've been delaying: _______________
2. What one micro-action can I take **today** to begin?
3. What lie have I been telling myself about this task?
4. What truth will I replace it with?

❖ **Affirmations:**

- "I take action before I feel ready."
- "Later is a lie—I move now."
- "Courage is my new starting point."

❖ **Journal Prompt:**

Write a letter to your future self, dated one year from today. Describe how taking small consistent actions has changed your life. Who have you become?

Chapter - 2
The Myth of Motivation

Motivation is a Result

Gokul stared at the motivational quote taped to his mirror: "Discipline equals freedom." He had written it in bold Sharpie three weeks ago, inspired by a podcast—but it no longer sparked anything.

He sighed and grabbed his toothbrush. Another day where his to-do list felt like a threat instead of a roadmap.

Later that morning, during their weekly call, Sunita asked him directly, "You haven't recorded your first podcast episode yet, have you?"

"I will. I just... haven't felt ready," he muttered.

There was silence on the line.

Then she replied, "You're still waiting for motivation, aren't you?"

He didn't answer. He didn't have to.

Sunita continued, "Motivation is the biggest scam we've ever bought into. You don't wait for motivation—you create it."

Gokul paced the room. "But what about those days when everything feels heavy? When you wake up tired, distracted, unmotivated?"

"That's when the magic happens," she said. "That's when you teach your brain that showing up isn't a feeling—it's a habit."

She challenged him: "This week, every time you want to 'feel ready' before starting, I want you to do the opposite. Start first. Let the motivation catch up to you."

Gokul laughed. "You want me to rebel against my instincts?"

"No," she replied. "I want you to lead them."

❖ **Key Insight:**

Motivation is not a prerequisite—it's a result. Waiting to feel inspired keeps you stuck; choosing action creates the energy you've been hoping for.

Lead Your Thoughts

Over the next few days, Gokul experimented.

Instead of waiting for inspiration, he gave himself a rule: "Start the task within five seconds of deciding to do it."

It was awkward at first. He'd open his laptop, heart racing, mind screaming, "This isn't the right time!" But he would whisper back, "Let's just start."

He found himself editing podcast notes before breakfast, writing outlines during lunch breaks, and surprisingly, enjoying it. Not because he felt driven—but because he felt proud.

One morning, he told Sunita, "I don't think I need motivation anymore."

She smiled. "You've upgraded."

"What do you mean?"

"You've shifted from feeling-driven to identity-driven," she said. "Now your question isn't 'Do I feel like it?'—it's 'What would the focused version of me do right now?'"

That night, Gokul wrote on a sticky note and posted it next to the quote on his mirror:
"Discipline is deciding in advance who you are."

The next day, he pressed "record" and spoke the first words of his new podcast:

"Welcome to The Now Habit. This is for everyone tired of waiting to feel ready. Let's begin anyway."

❖ **Key Insight:**

You don't need to feel motivated to take action—you need to act like the version of yourself who follows through. Discipline isn't punishment; it's self-leadership.

❖ **Worksheet: Flip the Script**

1. 1. Write one task you're waiting to feel motivated for.
2. 2. What action can you take on it right now, no matter your mood?
3. 3. What would the focused version of you do today?

❖ **Affirmations:**

- "I act before I feel ready."
- "Discipline is my true identity."
- "I lead my thoughts—they don't lead me."

❖ **Journal Prompt:**

Write about a time you waited for motivation and missed an opportunity. What could have changed if you had acted anyway?

Votes for Your Identity

By midweek, Gokul had found his rhythm—not a flawless one, but one grounded in consistency. Each morning started with a three-word mantra: "Begin, don't wait." It wasn't glamorous, but it worked.

One afternoon, he visited a coworking space downtown to escape the noise of home. He grabbed a desk near a window and laid out his journal, his laptop, and a sticky note that simply read: *"What would the focused me do now?"*

Two hours later, he had completed a podcast script, drafted an email to pitch his show to a mental health blog, and jotted down three episode ideas—all without waiting for a spark of inspiration.

During their next call, Sunita sounded proud. "See? You're not driven by feelings anymore. You're driven by commitment."

Gokul thought for a second. "But what if the commitment fades?"

"It won't," she said. "Because now you're not just doing tasks—you're building proof. Every time you show up, you're casting a vote for who you want to become."

The idea stuck with him: *small actions as identity votes.*

That night, he created a tracking system. Nothing complex—just a page with the title: *Votes for My Future*

Self. Each time he worked on something despite low motivation, he gave himself a tally.

The numbers began to add up. And with them, so did his confidence.

❖ **Key Insight:**

Every small action is a vote for the person you want to become. When consistency replaces perfection as your goal, self-trust begins to grow.

❖ **Worksheet: Cast Your Votes**

Create a page titled "Votes for My Future Self." Each time you act despite low motivation, mark a tally. Set a goal: "I will cast 10 identity votes this week."

❖ **Affirmations:**

- "Every small action is a vote for who I'm becoming."
- "I stay committed, even when feelings fade."
- "My discipline shapes my destiny."

❖ **Journal Prompt:**

What identity are you building through your actions? What is one vote you can cast today?

The Bounce-Back is the Breakthrough

By the weekend, Gokul faced his first real test. His schedule was tight, his energy low, and distractions high. The momentum he'd been building all week suddenly felt fragile.

He woke up late, skipped breakfast, and scrolled on his phone for nearly an hour. As the minutes slipped by, guilt crept in. The old narrative returned: See? You can't stay consistent.

But instead of surrendering, he opened his journal and stared at his *"Votes for My Future Self"* page. It wasn't full yet—but it wasn't empty either.

"I need a reset," he muttered.

He turned to a blank page and wrote the words: *"Bounce Back Blueprint."*

Here's what he wrote:
1. *Name what happened. (I got distracted and broke my morning routine.)*
2. *Neutralize the guilt. (Everyone slips. One day doesn't erase my effort.)*
3. *Restart small. (What can I do in the next 10 minutes to get back on track?)*
4. *Reaffirm identity. (This slip is proof that I'm growing, not failing.)*

Gokul chose a 10-minute focus session. He put his phone on airplane mode, brewed coffee, and outlined the second episode of his podcast. It wasn't perfect—but it was something.

Later, when he told Sunita, she clapped. "That," she said, "wasn't motivation. That was muscle."

He realized then that the true measure of progress isn't how perfectly we perform—but how quickly we return.

That night, he added a new quote beside his mirror:

"The bounce-back is the breakthrough."

❖ **Key Insight:**

True transformation comes not from doing everything right, but from learning how to recover quickly, gently, and without judgment.

"I showed up to workout five days last week. First time in months. I agree, your mantra sure work" she said with accomplishment and excitement.

"That's really great. Glad to be of help" Gokul replied and thought in mind *'One small conversation. One ripple'*.

The Momentum Map

Sunita called him that Sunday. "I read a study," she said excitedly, "that says our brain releases dopamine not when we complete a task—but when we *start* one."

Gokul blinked. "So I've been rewarding myself this whole time without realizing?"

"Exactly," she laughed. "The trick is to lower the entry barrier so much that starting feels effortless."

They talked for an hour about the science of behavior. She told him about BJ Fogg's "Tiny Habits" model—where transformation begins not with 30-day plans, but with brushing your teeth and doing one push-up.

"You're not changing your life in one decision," she said. "You're building a compound effect. One win, one moment at a time."

That week, Gokul created a chart titled *The Momentum Map*. He listed five areas of life—Health, Work, Home, Relationships, and Creativity—and set a single, ultra-simple micro-win for each one.

Example:
- **Health:** Stretch for 2 minutes after waking.
- **Work:** Reply to one email before lunch.
- **Home:** Wash 5 dishes before dinner.
- **Relationships:** Send one "thinking of you" message.
- **Creativity:** Write one sentence of a podcast script.

The Progress Ritual

By Sunday evening, Gokul felt lighter—not because everything was perfect, but because he had finally stopped tying his worth to his productivity.

He sat on his rooftop with a cup of tea and his journal in hand, writing a letter to his future self.

"You didn't need more motivation," he wrote. *"You needed to trust that progress comes from doing, not waiting."*

Then he flipped the page and wrote his own version of a manifesto:
- *I don't wait for perfect moods.*
- *I don't chase inspiration.*
- *I build myself, moment by moment.*
- *I choose discipline over delay.*
- *I am who I consistently act like.*

This was more than a habit now. It was a philosophy.

A few weeks ago, he had been the guy who waited for the stars to align. Now, he was becoming someone who acted anyway. The podcast was underway, his confidence was rising, and his patterns were changing.

He knew setbacks would come again. But he also knew this: *motivation might start a fire, but it's discipline that keeps it burning.*

<table><tr><td>

❖ **Key Insight:**

Daily rituals tied to your desired identity can serve as anchors, reminding you who you're choosing to be—not just what you're trying to do.

</td></tr></table>

❖ **Transformation Plan:**
The Bounce-Back Blueprint
  Use this when you slip:
  1. What happened?
  2. What story am I telling myself about it?
  3. What small action can I take next?
  4. What truth can I choose to believe now?

❖ **Affirmations:**

  - "I bounce back stronger."
  - "Every action is a choice toward who I want to be."
  - "I am not my mistakes—I am my recovery."

❖ **Journal Prompt:**

Describe your latest setback. How did you respond? What identity did your response reflect—and what would you like it to reflect next time?

Chapter - 3
Micro Wins, Massive Results

Forward is Forward

The gym smelled of rubber mats and determination. Gokul stood at the entrance, scanning the weight racks and treadmill stations. He hadn't stepped foot in a gym in months—not since his brief New Year's resolution fizzled out in February.

This time was different.

He wasn't here for a transformation montage. He was here for *five* minutes.

Sunita had planted the idea. "Forget the hour-long workouts," she told him. "Your brain needs proof that you're someone who shows up—not someone who does it all."

So he did.

Five minutes on the bike. That's it.

As he pedaled, something unexpected happened: the guilt started to fade. He wasn't behind. He wasn't broken. He was in motion.

Next to him on a treadmill, a woman about his age was stretching out. She glanced at his sticky note taped to his phone: *"Five minutes counts."*

"Is that your mantra?" she asked, smiling.

He nodded. "Yep. Just doing what I can today."

"Wow. That's quite interesting" she said. "I'm Aria, by the way" she continued "I think I can use this mantra too".

"I'm Gokul and you can, for sure, use this method. It works." Gokul replied with a smile.

That evening, he wrote in his journal: *"Five minutes counts. Forward is forward."*

This realization—that *"micro wins carry massive weight"*—became his new mantra.

He started using it everywhere:
- Five minutes writing a podcast script.
- One drawer cleaned in his cluttered kitchen.
- Two push-ups before bed.
- One email answered.

Each micro win was a message to his brain: *We are building momentum.*

By the end of the week, Gokul wasn't just more productive—he was more peaceful. He wasn't racing the clock. He was owning it, moment by moment.

The next week in the Gym, Aria waved from across the room.

What shocked him was how these small steps began to chain together.

Two minutes of stretching became five. One sentence of writing became a paragraph. One clean dish turned into a spotless kitchen.

Micro became momentum.

And momentum became identity.

He was no longer chasing massive overhauls. He was building a sustainable rhythm.

As he reviewed his notes that night, Gokul got a message from Sunita:

"You've got me thinking. I haven't blogged in six months, but watching you commit to small daily actions—well, I wrote something today. Didn't plan to. Just started."

He smiled, realizing something powerful: *his progress was permission*—not just for himself, but for others.

❖ **Key Insight:**

Breaking life into tiny, achievable actions reduces overwhelm and helps you build cross-domain momentum that reinforces your sense of agency.

❖ **Worksheet: Build Your Momentum Map**

Choose 5 life areas. For each, set a micro-action that takes less than 5 minutes. Commit to doing each daily for 7 days.

❖ **Affirmations:**

- "Micro actions create macro impact."
- "Momentum is built in small moments."
- "Starting is success."

❖ **Journal Prompt:**

What area of your life feels stuck? What is one ridiculously small action you could take today to begin shifting it?

One napkin at a time.

On Wednesday evening, Gokul met up with his old college friend Rishi at a coffee shop. They hadn't seen each other in months, and the moment Rishi slouched into the seat, Gokul could see the storm in his eyes.

"Man, I don't know what's wrong with me," Rishi said, rubbing his face. "I've got all these plans, this app idea, a freelance gig, even a blog I started... and nothing's moving. I just feel stuck."

Gokul nodded, remembering that feeling well.

"I used to think I needed to push harder," Rishi continued, "but I'm just tired. All the time."

Gokul leaned back, sipped his coffee, and smiled.

"What if you didn't need to push harder?" he said. "What if you needed to start smaller?"

Rishi frowned. "Smaller?"

Gokul pulled a napkin and pen from the side of the table. "What's one thing you could do in five minutes that moves *any* of those things forward?"

Rishi thought for a moment. "Maybe... outline one section of my app pitch?"

"Perfect," Gokul said, scribbling on the napkin:

Small Action = Energy = Progress.

Then he drew a loop:

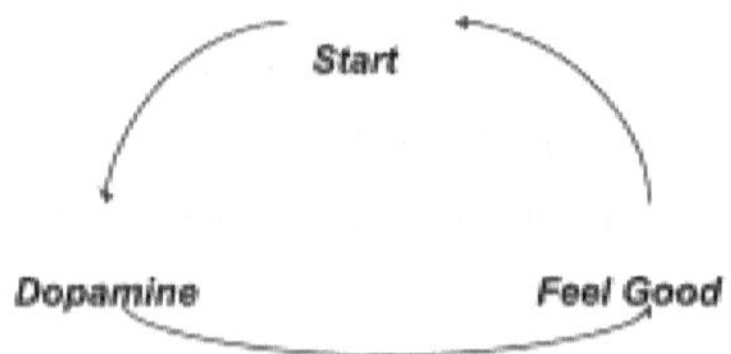

"This is what saved me," he said. "Not doing more—just proving to myself that I *do*. Micro wins. They multiply."

Rishi stared at the napkin, then chuckled. "You sound like some kind of anti-procrastination coach."

"Maybe I am," Gokul laughed. "One napkin at a time."

<hr>

❖   **Key Insight:**

Your habits don't just change you—they give permission and inspiration to others. Even small wins can ripple outward.

Micro wins, repeated, become new baselines. When they're consistent, your identity shifts from effort to ease.

The Ripple Effect.

The next morning, Gokul opened his inbox to find an email from Rishi.

Subject: *"It works."*

The body read:

"Outlined the pitch. Didn't overthink it. Just five minutes like you said. Felt good. Did another five. Sent it to a mentor. Got feedback. Man, this micro stuff is magic."

Gokul grinned and typed back:

"Told you. Momentum multiplies."

Then he flipped to the back of his journal and created a new section: *"The Ripple Effect."*

He listed the names of people he had helped simply by showing up, by sharing his journey.

- Sunita (inspired to start her own blog series)

- Aria (from his gym, started stretching daily after his encouragement)

- Rishi (launched pitch)

One person's micro wins had become someone else's breakthrough.

He wrote:

"Every step I take invites someone else to move."

And maybe that was the biggest result of all—not what he accomplished, but who he inspired to rise alongside him.

❖ **Key Insight:**

The most powerful legacy of behavior change isn't the results—it's the people you help create change through your quiet consistency.

❖ **Worksheet: The Ripple Effect Tracker**

List three people who might benefit from seeing your micro wins. What's one small way you can share your momentum with them this week?

❖ **Affirmations:**

- "My actions are invitations."

- "Small steps create waves."

- "Momentum is contagious."

❖ **Journal Prompt:**

Who in your life could benefit from seeing you take action? How can your consistency become someone else's inspiration?

Chapter - 4
Your Future Self Is Waiting

Start now, live forward

Gokul sat cross-legged on the carpet, the evening light spilling through his blinds. The room was still. Outside, a distant siren wailed, but in here, time had slowed. In his lap, his journal lay open to a blank page titled: *"Future Self Visualization."*

He took a deep breath. Sunita's challenge echoed in his mind: "Close your eyes. Imagine it's a year from now. You've become the best version of yourself. What do you look like? What does your day feel like?"

He hesitated—part of him afraid. What if he couldn't see anything? What if nothing had changed?

But he forced his eyes shut.

Slowly, a figure took shape in his imagination. Himself—but lighter. Not physically, but emotionally. He stood taller. His movements were intentional, unhurried. His clothes were simple, neat. His skin glowed—not from sunlight, but from a quiet sense of peace.

Future Gokul sat across from him, smiling gently.

"I'm not perfect," he said, "but I'm consistent."

Gokul asked, "How did you get here?"

"One honest decision at a time. I stopped procrastinating and started showing up."

"You're not as far as you think," Future Gokul continued.

"I've just made different choices more often."

Gokul, now, asked a series of questions,

"What do you do first thing in the morning?"

"I move my body." future Gokul replied.

"What don't you do?"

"I don't negotiate with my excuses." future Gokul replied.

"How did you become... you?"

"I kept promises when no one else was watching." future Gokul replied.

Gokul slowly opened his eyes with tears brimming and scribbled across the page. He felt... steadier. The vision didn't make everything easy—but it made things *clear* that

"He's not waiting to be found—he's waiting to be built."

❖ **Key Insight:**

Your future self isn't imaginary—it's a version of you built by today's decisions. Visualization reveals who you want to become.

Aligned Rituals

Later that week, Gokul shared the experience with Sunita during a walk through a park covered in golden coloured leaves.

"I saw him," he said. "My future self. He was calm. Clear. Like someone who didn't need to hustle anymore because he trusted himself."

Sunita nodded, kicking at a pile of leaves. "And what does he do every day?"

Gokul didn't even pause. "He writes before checking his phone. Walks. Eats slowly. Finishes what he starts. Speaks gently to himself. He has boundaries. Not rigid ones—just ones rooted in love."

She turned to face him. "You know the difference between who you are and who he is?"

He smiled. "My habits."

"That's it," she said. "He's not an idea. He's just you, lived consistently."

That night, Gokul created a two-column list in his journal:
- Current Self Rituals — hit snooze, scroll phone, half-eat breakfast
- Future Self Rituals — wake on time, stretch, write three lines, eat mindfully

He circled the second column, writing beside it: *"Start now, live forward."*

❖ **Key Insight:**

You don't find your purpose—you build alignment. The habits of your future self are the road to becoming them.

You ever met your future self?

On Saturday, he met Aria in a quiet bookstore cafe. She was restless, sipping her coffee too quickly, fingers tapping her cup.

"I'm tired of living in drafts," she blurted. "Draft poems. Draft plans. Draft versions of myself."

Gokul tilted his head. "You ever met your future self?"

She raised an eyebrow. "Sounds like a guided meditation ad."

He grinned, pulling out his notebook and flipping to the visualization page. "It's weird at first. But powerful. Try it."

She closed her eyes reluctantly. "Okay, I see... me. But she's taller. Clear-eyed. Wears a blazer, ha! She's... signing books? Holy crap."

They both laughed, but her voice cracked. "I want to be her so badly."

Gokul leaned forward. "Then you start doing her rituals. What's one thing Future Aria does daily?"

"Reads poetry before bed," she whispered.

"Then do it tonight. That's the bridge."

She hugged him before leaving. "You're becoming someone, Gokul. I can feel it."

He watched her walk away and thought: Maybe this is who I was meant to be all along—not perfect, but contagious.

❖ **Key Insight:**

We're all drafts of who we want to be. The bridge to confidence is showing up today like the version we envision.

Letter from My Future Self

That night, Gokul opened his journal to a fresh page titled: "Letter from My Future Self."

He wrote:

Dear Gokul,

You kept your promises when no one else was watching.
You chose alignment over approval.
You walked every morning even when the sky was grey.
You didn't skip your voice—you found it.
You wrote. You showed up. You became.

When he finished, he stared at the letter. It felt like a handshake across time.

Then, with a deep breath, he pulled out an old to-do list from the back of the notebook. It was crumpled, smudged, covered in panic scribbles. He held it in his hands, then gently tore it in half.

Not with anger—but with respect.

"I needed that version of me," he whispered. "But I don't need his map anymore."

❖ **Key Insight:**

Writing from your future self's voice helps pull identity forward, making growth feel real before it arrives.

Every Step Closes the Gap

The next morning, Gokul stood in front of the mirror, toothbrush in one hand, sticky note in the other.

He pressed the note onto the glass. It read: "Act like the man you're becoming."

This became his ritual:
1. Morning wins reflection
2. One "Future Self" question: What would he do today?
3. One micro-action to honor it

4. One sentence of self-respect: "I'm proud of how I showed up."

Later that week, he bumped into Aria at the gym. She pointed to her phone lock screen—a quote: "Future me will thank me for this."

"You started something," she said.

He smiled. "So did you."

As he walked home, the city buzzing around him, he felt a new sense of stillness inside. His future self wasn't a stranger anymore.

He was in motion. Every step forward was a form of remembrance. Every act of discipline was a reunion.

And every morning was a chance to close the gap.

❖ **Key Insight:**

By acting as if you're already the future version of yourself, each day becomes a step across the divide.

❖ **Future Self Blueprint Worksheet**

- Write a letter from your Future Self (1 year later).
- What did you achieve? What did you let go of?
- What habits carried you here?
- What truth do you now live by?

❖ **Affirmations:**

- "My future is shaped by my present patterns."
- "Every decision is a vote for my evolution."
- "I act like the person I'm becoming."

❖ **Journal Prompt:**

Close your eyes. See your best self. What's one routine they do that you can start today?

Chapter - 5

The Comeback Blueprint

Pause, Don't Delete

Rain drummed softly against Gokul's window as he stared at the blinking cursor on his screen. For the first time in weeks, he felt disconnected. The momentum, the rituals, the clarity—they all felt distant.

He hadn't journaled in three days. His podcast drafts sat untouched. He'd scrolled mindlessly for hours the night before. That tight grip of guilt returned, whispering: "See? It was all a phase."

Sunita called. "Rough week?" she asked, gently.

"I lost the thread," he admitted.

"No, you dropped the thread. And now you get to pick it back up."

She reminded him of something she once heard: "You're allowed to pause. Just don't delete your progress."

That line stuck.

Later, Gokul sat down and opened his journal. At the top of the page he wrote: *"Blueprint to Bounce Back."*

He listed:

1. *Name what happened. (I avoided, I numbed, I disconnected.)*
2. *Own the emotion without judgment. (Guilt, shame, fatigue.)*
3. *Rebuild with grace. (What one act can remind me who I am?)*
4. *Recommit. (Start again—not because I failed, but because I'm growing.)*

He didn't fix everything that day. But he showed up. And that changed everything.

❖ **Key Insight:**

Falling off course isn't failure. Guilt fades when you learn to restart with compassion and honesty.

Rebuild Softly

The next morning, he stepped outside despite the drizzle and walked around the block. No podcast playing. No agenda. Just movement.

Each step whispered, "I'm back."

Later, he spoke with Aria again. She'd hit her own wall—overcommitted, overwhelmed, and questioning her passion.

"I haven't written in over a week," she said.

Gokul smiled. "That's okay. Want to try something together?"

They sat down with notebooks. Each wrote a Comeback Letter to themselves.

Dear Me,
It's okay to fall. It's human to retreat. But you've never once let that be the end. This pause doesn't erase your power. Start small. Start kind. Just start.

Tears welled in Aria's eyes. "Why does this feel so heavy and healing?"

"Because we never learned to return gently," Gokul said. "We only learned to restart through guilt."

That day, they promised to rebuild softly, like artists—not soldiers.

❖ **Key Insight:**

Writing a letter to yourself after a setback invites grace and forgiveness—core ingredients for sustainable self-leadership.

The Comeback Tracker

By midweek, Gokul created a tool he called The Comeback Tracker.

Each time he returned after slipping—a walk, a note, a five-minute task—he'd mark a check.

What surprised him? Those days, though "off," still created momentum. Recovery wasn't a setback. It was a skill.

He noticed something: the more he tracked comebacks, the fewer "off days" lingered.

One day he shared it with Rishi, who was drowning in freelance burnout.

"I missed two deadlines. I feel like a fraud," Rishi confessed.

"Then your comeback's about to be epic," Gokul said. "Track it. One act. One mark. That's all."

Rishi tried it. Three days later, he called and said, "I feel like I'm winning again. Even when I mess up."

That night, Gokul wrote in his journal: *"The strength isn't in never slipping—it's in trusting my return."*

RRR - Reflect, Reframe, Restart

Gokul began to teach what he was learning.

In a small online workshop he hosted for listeners of his podcast, he introduced the 3R Comeback Framework:

1. **Reflect** – What pulled you off course?
2. **Reframe** – What is this teaching me?
3. **Restart** – What's one small action I can do now?

He walked the group through it with gentle prompts and music in the background.

One participant typed in the chat: *"This is the first time I've forgiven myself for pausing."*

Another: *"I didn't realize how often I quit just because I slipped."*

Gokul looked at the screen of names, his heart full. He wasn't just bouncing back. He was helping others return to themselves.

That night, Sunita messaged him: *"You've turned your stumbles into steps for others. I'm proud of you."*

He replied: *"Every comeback has the power to carry someone else too."*

❖   **Key Insight:**

Your comeback story isn't just yours—it can be a tool, a teaching, and a light for others.

Persistence > perfection

The end of the month arrived. Gokul reviewed his calendar, journal, and Comeback Tracker. There were gaps. Imperfections. Crossed-out entries.

But also: Growth. Grace. Grit.

He realized something powerful—he didn't fear failure anymore. Because now he knew how to come back, come home.

In the final page of his journal, he wrote his Comeback Manifesto:

- I will fall. That's human.
- I will rise. That's growth.
- I will return. That's identity.
- I will not confuse pauses with failure.
- I will not let shame write my story.

He placed the manifesto above his desk.

When he pressed "upload" on his latest podcast episode, he whispered aloud,

"This isn't perfection. This is persistence."

And in that, he found peace.

❖   **Key Insight:**

The real victory isn't staying on track perfectly—it's rewriting your story every time you return with courage.

❖ **Comeback Blueprint Worksheet**

1. What pulled me off track?
2. What story am I telling myself about it?
3. What truth can I tell instead?
4. What one small action can I take today?

❖ **Affirmations:**

- "I return with grace."
- "Every pause is a chance to reset."
- "Comebacks are my superpower."

❖ **Journal Prompt:**

Describe a moment you slipped. How did you respond then? How do you choose to respond now?

**Take the First Step to UNSTUCK and Become the
Person You Were Meant to Be**

THE END